floral gifts

floral gifts

creating flower-filled gifts for every occasion

Jacky Hobbs

photography by Michelle Garrett

RYLAND
PETERS
& SMALL

LONDON NEW YORK

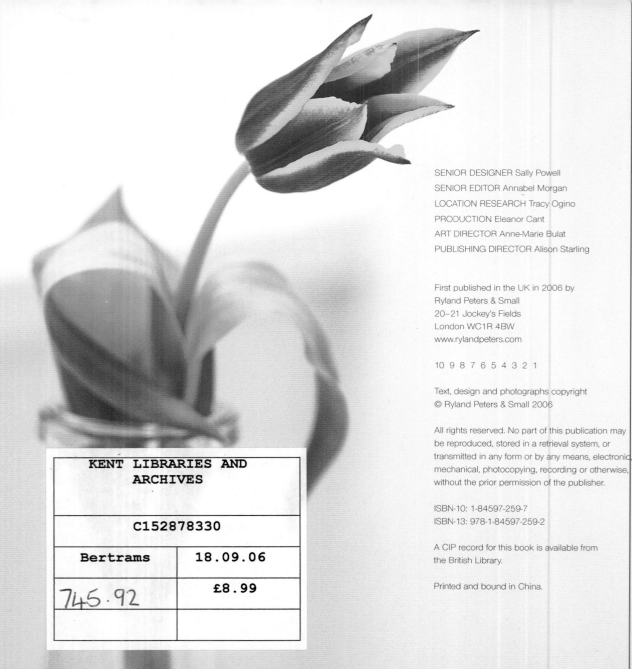

SENIOR DESIGNER Sally Powell
SENIOR EDITOR Annabel Morgan
LOCATION RESEARCH Tracy Ogino
PRODUCTION Eleanor Cant
ART DIRECTOR Anne-Marie Bulat
PUBLISHING DIRECTOR Alison Starling

First published in the UK in 2006 by
Ryland Peters & Small
20–21 Jockey's Fields
London WC1R 4BW
www.rylandpeters.com

10 9 8 7 6 5 4 3 2 1

ISBN-10: 1-84597-259-7
ISBN-13: 978-1-84597-259-2

A CIP record for this book is available from
the British Library.

Printed and bound in China.

contents

introduction

Fabulous flowers need little introduction, but in *Floral Gifts* we are aiming for the extraordinary. This can only be achieved by combining beautiful flowers and plants with clever containers – a unique combination that enables you to create unforgettable and personal gifts.

When it comes to choosing a container for your floral offering, think creatively. Absolutely anything that has a hole in can be filled with flowers. For girl friends, femininity rules, opening doors for unusual containers such as handbags or hatboxes. A friend's favourite hobby might inspire you to choose a particular item, while, as for men – well, that's a whole different challenge!

Every container has an inherent character of its own, which you can play up when it comes to the planting. Wicker, wood and basketware – in the form of wreaths, bird feeders, birdcages and tool holders – all have rustic connotations and are suited to delicate bulbs or country-garden blooms. Metal containers can be contemporary and masculine. Cubes and boxes call for simple, bold plantings, while classical, elegant urns offer opportunities for more traditional offerings. Alternatively, galvanized metal watering cans and pails seem to cry out for a relaxed jumble of country-garden flowers.

Fling open your cupboard doors to find an Aladdin's cave of innovative containers – baking tins, colanders and jelly moulds. Search out glassware – tiny tea-light holders, storm lanterns, milk bottles, and even perfume bottles for an especially fragrant posy. Vintage china is also wonderful – jugs, mismatching cups and saucers, soup tureens and chamber pots. Whatever your fancy, fill it with flowers to create a unique gift for someone special.

looking good

The following tips will ensure floral arrangements that are both long-lasting and beautiful:

- Containers must be watertight, so line baskets, old china or metal objects with florist's cellophane or thick black plastic, secured with florist's tape.
- 'Fit' awkward shapes with secondary, concealed waterproof vessels such as plastic bowls or glass jars.
- Use chicken wire to hold flowers in shape, as it can be moulded to fit any container, creating a framework for your flowers. Simply snip and bend into shape.

- Flowers should always be freshly cut, and free of any foliage below the water line.
- Plants need to be kept in an appropriate medium. If shop-bought, you may be able to leave them in their pots and top-dress them with a decorative mulch – small stones, gravel, bark, moss or petals.
- Glass or wicker containers can leave ugly 'foundations' exposed. Line baskets with moss or set pots into petal-filled glassware. (Rose petals or lavender seeds are great.)
- Gift wrap – wrap in decorative paper, adorn with streamers or ribbon, or cover with sheaths of tissue paper.

colour, texture and finishing touches

A successful marriage relies on harmony between partners. It's the same for flowers and their containers: empathy is essential – strike the right chord and the whole will be greater than the sum of its parts!

- Use complementary, harmonious colours to gentle effect, or contrasting colours for more striking results. (Remember: opposites attract too!)

- When using patterned or decorated containers, choose flowers that somehow echo or tie in with the design.

- Use the textural qualities of the flowers to subtle advantage. For example, you could match the papery sheaths of paper whites to the pages of an antique book (see page 58), while fringed, open-throated tulips will feather an Easter nest perfectly (see page 18).

use contrasting colours
for more striking effects

● Match up container and flowers for the right effect – defined geometric lines denote a more masculine look, as shown with cacti (see page 42), while soft fabrics and gentle curves lend themselves to more romantic effects, such as knitted baby bootees filled with dainty ranunculi (see page 17).

● If possible, 'say it with flowers' – any Jack would be chuffed to bits with *Agapanthus* 'Jack's Blue' , while surely any Poppy, Daisy or Rose would welcome a vintage teacup filled with their namesake blooms.

Strike a personal note that recalls a shared memory, and your gift will assume that intended special meaning.

special occasions

valentine's day

Heart to heart A heart-shaped basket looks irresistible planted with spring bulbs. Valentine's day is a wonderful opportunity to send flowers with meaning to your beloved, and even the frostiest heart will melt when greeted with 'Hearts Desire' tulips in shades of peach and cream.

Other flowers with romantic connotations, such as dark-eyed forget-me-nots, would also work well. The basket has been lined with thick plastic, which is concealed with a thin layer of moss. Pack the container with bulb fibre, then plant the bulbs individually in the fibre and decorate with ribbon.

Fragile and shy, the snowdrop epitomizes true love, its tiny green heart emblazoned on its pure white sleeve for all to see. This arrangement of dainty spring snowdrops is a delicate romantic gesture, full of charm, and all the more meaningful for its diminutive stature.

Vintage French silvered cheese moulds have been used as containers here, but they could easily be replaced with other small heart-shaped containers, such as tea-light holders or miniature cake tins. Each one has been planted with a cluster of emerging snowdrops packed into the containers with handfuls of wood bark shavings. Wait and watch as they throw back their outer petals to reveal a perfect painted heart, the symbol of true love. Keep them cool, and you will be able to cherish their amorous display longer than any forced rose.

new baby

Celebrate a friend or family's new arrival with a small gift filled with flowers. The gift should be something to treasure and cherish – just like the tiny recipient!

Keepsake gift Choose a traditional christening gift such as a silver christening cup, an egg cup or a silver first-tooth holder and fill it with a handful of sweet-scented flowers. If the container has a wide opening, arrange the flowers in a submerged 'cap' of fine chicken wire or a chunk of water-saturated Oasis to keep the posy secure.

Pick rosy pink blooms for a girl – part-unfurled rosebuds, ranunculi or frilly sweet peas

Bootiful babies Irresistible tiny knitted bootees are a classic new baby gift. Instead of stuffing them with tissue to hold their form, these bootees each contain a glass tea-light holder that acts as a miniature vase and holds a dainty hand-tied posy. Half-fill each glass holder with water and arrange a tiny beribboned bouquet of flowers inside each one. Now, carefully insert a glass holder containing a posy into each tiny bootee.

Pick rosy pink blooms for a girl – part-unfurled rosebuds, satin-petalled ranunculi or frilly sweet peas. For a boy, choose gentle pastelly blues – campanulas or bluebells. Alternatively, opt for ever-popular whites – clusters of snowy-white lilac, or frothy gypsophila.

In some cases, you may even be able to offer appropriately named flowers, such as *Agapanthus* 'Jack's Blue', for example, or simply roses, daisies or poppies for baby girls bearing flower names.

easter celebration

What better way to celebrate Easter than with fabulous flower-filled Easter baskets?

An Easter nest is packed with palest pink frilled-edge tulips that almost seem to be chirping like hungry chicks. Continue the nest theme by poking pretty speckled feathers, darker pink wax flowers and tiny quail's eggs into the twiggy nest. Similar nests can be found at florists or craft shops, or you could cover the outside of a round basket with slender twigs before planting it up with spring bulbs. Alternatively, as shown, fill the

nest with pretty cut flowers. Place a circle of glass tea-light holders within the empty nest, half-fill each holder with water, and then place two or three stems in each vessel to ensure an evenly filled effect.

An Easter egg hunt in a basket is a fun-filled gift for a friend with a sweet tooth. This arrangement packs all the ingredients for a traditional Easter egg hunt together in a pretty rustic basket. Line a wicker basket with thick plastic before filling it with bulb fibre and planting it up with a combination of spring bulbs and flowers, including sunny yellow daffodils, delicate primroses and tiny crocuses. Cover over the surface with springy moss and scatter clusters of miniature foil-covered chocolate eggs around the base of the foliage and flowers.

velvety, **aromatic** chocolate cosmos
really do smell of chocolate!

birthday bouquets

Chocoholic's delight Chocolate-scented flowers are a clever twist on the classic fall-back birthday gift of a box of chocolates. Here, a glossy heart-shaped box has been filled with velvety, aromatic chocolate cosmos – and they really do smell of chocolate! Find a low waterproof container that fits in the box and stuff it with scrumpled chicken wire. Half-fill with water, then arrange your flowers. Tie the box with ribbon for a calorie-free gift.

Light up someone's day with this arrangement of candles and calla lilies in a glass storm lantern. Pour a small amount of water into the bottom of the lantern, and arrange yellow and pink calla lily stems around the central candle holder, ensuring the bottoms of their stems are in the water. Place tapered candles in matching hues in the central candle holder. Wrap the base of the lantern with coloured tissue, and tie with jolly streamers.

The icing on the cake Create a birthday cake with a difference – a flower-bedecked cake stand, complete with candles for the all-essential birthday wish.

Simple, pretty pressed-glass cake stands are available from antique or kitchen shops. This one has been adorned with colourful glass tea-light holders, arranged in a loose circle with one holder at the centre. Each of the outer glass holders has been filled with a small bouquet of fragrant freesias in jewelled colours that match the holders. The central holder contains a handful of slender tapers. The result is a fragrant centrepiece for the birthday table. And, of course, the glass cake stand and tea-light holders can be used over and over again.

Gift box to go This smart arrangement is a flower-filled version of a classic ribbon-tied gift box – an eye-catching present with instant appeal. The contemporary, cubic lines of this square metal vase call for an equally clean and contemporary approach to the flowers. For dramatic effect, use a mass of a single flower type – anemones in tones of midnight blue or saturated velvety red. Large flower heads, like gerbera, poppies or dahlias, all massed together and held in a chicken wire frame, create a fabulous sense of generous abundance, whilst completely covering the vase opening.

Tape a strip of broad ribbon, matching the flowers' colours, to each side of the cube, and your floral gift is all wrapped and ready to go.

christmas

Create seasonal floral wreaths and festive centrepieces to give as gifts or to enjoy yourself.

A Christmas wreath, rich with bright berries and velvety roses, extends a special welcome to guests. A simple twig wreath, from a floral supply shop, was dressed up for the season with gauzy red ribbon and glossy rosehips and berries. The trimmed wreath was then studded with ruby-red roses and ornamental cabbages. The stems are placed in water-filled plastic florist's vials that have been wired to the back of the wreath.

Yule log The Christmas rose, *Helleborus niger*, looks exquisite in a silver-birch bark-covered container, trimmed with fir sprigs and candles. The delicacy of the flowers is emphasized by the glass bell cloche that covers the arrangement.

gifts for girls

bags of style

Feminine frills or smart and structured – a handbag is truly a girl's best friend. When giving a bag as a gift, dress it up with fresh flowers before it's given over to general clutter.

Choose a bag that reflects your friend's style and personality. Neat and tidy types will appreciate a compact bag and a simple arrangement, while girly girls will adore a more whimsical offering in soft and gentle tones, such as the creamy pompom-headed white hydrangeas in the floppy felt bag shown above.

To hold the flowers, take a plastic container, pack in a piece of chicken wire, half-fill the container with water and arrange the blooms. When you are happy with the arrangement, carefully place the container into the base of the bag.

Bathtime treats Give a girl friend the ultimate floral treat –
a bouquet of fragrant herbs for her to enjoy in the calm
sanctuary of a candlelit bathroom.

Lavender is well-known for its soothing qualities, so is ideal
for a relaxing spa-style bath. Dress up potted lavender plants
from the local garden centre in pretty containers – a vintage-
style enamelled metal bucket, or a plastic lined rustic linen
sack. Don't forget to add some lavender-scented soap,
aromatherapy oil or bath salts. The fresh flowerheads can be
sprinkled into the bath, and the plants can be kept in the
bathroom, where the steamy atmosphere will encourage
the herbs to release their aromatic scent.

camomile, mint
lemon verbena and rosemary

afternoon tea

An invitation to afternoon tea, that most civilized of traditions, demands a charming floral gift. For a tea lover, an antique china teapot filled with an aromatic bunch of freshly cut, tea-making herbs is a thoughtful offering. The recipient can pluck camomile, mint or lemon verbena from the pot to create fragrant infusions. A tea strainer, with a note tucked within, makes a perfect gift tag.

Ladylike china tea and coffee cups (above) planted with dainty, diminutive blooms make demure and charmingly old-fashioned gifts, ideal for visits to grandmothers, aunts or other relatives. Buy potted violets, rose pink kalanchoe (shown) or campanulas, and replant them in dainty, mismatching antique-shop cups and saucers. Conceal the soil with a layer of verdant moss.

delight your hostess with a thoughtful gesture

dressing for dinner

Taking flowers to a dinner party can be a chore for a busy hostess, who has to drop everything to arrange them in water. Instead, delight her with an elegant centrepiece for her dining table. Find a vegetable tureen or sauce boat that harmonizes with her dinner service, then dress it up with fresh flowers. Shape a piece of chicken wire into a slightly curved dome and pop it into the container to hold the flowers in place. Choose blooms that complement the colour and style of the container.

For a kitchen-table supper, pop single blooms into glass bottles and slot them into a decorative wire carrier. Here (left), tulips and alstroemeria make for a relaxed ensemble and could be separated to create individual floral place settings.

mother's day

Mother's Day gifts are an opportunity to make your mother feel loved and appreciated. It doesn't have to be a grand gesture, but it should be a thoughtful, personal gift. And whatever you give her, try to include her favourite flowers.

Hats off to mum For a Mother's Day gift, flowers may be a given, but you also need to make the container count. Think of a unique way to display your flowers, or find a wonderful container and then choose flowers to suit. This fabulous bouquet of deep-pink, richly scented lilies (above) is presented in a lucky junk-shop find – an antique Victorian hatbox.

First arrange your bouquet of lilies in a low glass vase, using chicken wire to hold them firmly in place. Just before presenting the arrangement, place the vase in the hatbox.

My old china Who could resist an arrangement of pretty old china jugs? You could be adding to an existing collection, or providing inspiration for the future. Whether arranged individually or together, these jugs will add a soft and feminine note to any interior. The copper lustre of these jugs lends itself to hot, bold tones – ranunculus blooms in lipstick pink, deep burgundy and coppery red. Just a few pretty flowers in the right vessel will turn heads and move hearts, so choose carefully and give with love.

gifts for guys

wine and fruit

Wine lover Men can be so difficult to buy for, especially when it comes to flowers. The usual tied bunch or pretty posy just isn't suitable. Instead, when giving flowers to a man, try to find an interest, an edge, an angle. For a wine lover, why not research your man's preferred wines, and put your knowledge to good use? Create his very own mini vineyard, in the shape of an authentic wooden wine crate packed with a generous cluster of wine-producing grapes (still on the vine, if possible), flowers in a toning shade, and, of course, a bottle of his favourite wine. This is a substantial and, most important, masculine gift, which will bring hours of enjoyment to the recipient.

The way to a man's heart is through his stomach,
or so the saying goes. And even if that isn't the case, what
man could resist this delectable, portable fruit garden, brimming
with glossy, ruby-red strawberries and plump figs, ripe for the picking?

The key to this arrangement is the decorative French fruit basket that
houses the plants. Search antique stores or kitchen shops for similar
versions. Arrange potted strawberry plants and a potted fig in the basket,
and decorate with a punnet of ripe berries – a taste of things to come.
The pots can then be lifted out for planting.

desktop delights

While a bunch of flowers doesn't always feel appropriate for a man, bulbs or branches go down a treat. Colour is important – blue, purple, green and burgundy all work well. Give special thought to the actual planting, seeking containers with a masculine edge.

Bulb-filled letter rack An antique letter rack is a perfect gift, as well as the ideal receptacle for neat little rows of spring bulbs. The bold outlines of *Iris reticulata* 'George' (left) make it a striking candidate. Line the letter rack with plastic liner or clingfilm before half-filling the slots with bulb fibre. Place ready-to-flower bulbs in rows as desired, then conceal the fibre with coloured stones. Add a narrow ribbon if you dare!

Inkwell vase A single crocus bulb held in a vintage glass inkwell will bring a splash of colour and a hint of springtime to any desk, and can double up as a paperweight.

cacti and topiary

Architectural elements go down well with men. Plants with structure and form, like neatly ordered topiary and spiny cacti, will fit the bill perfectly.

Cowboy's cactus A row of spiny little specimens creates the perfect miniature desert garden, perfect for a windowsill or desk. Here, a selection of cacti in a variety of different shapes was planted up in a row of chic galvanized metal cubes. The soil was covered with fine gravel to complete the chic minimalist effect.

Tabletop topiary A miniature evergreen myrtle planted in a classical metal urn makes for a stately gift. Give a ready-trimmed standard, or provide a plant and a wire frame and topiary shears, so your man can therapeutically snip pyramids, obelisks or other shapes to his heart's content.

themed gifts

bird lover

Birdcages and bird feeders make wonderfully decorative hanging gardens, indoors and out.

Oriental pavilion Place a simple potted orchid in a decorative, oriental-style wooden or metal birdcage. Encourage the flowers to peep beguilingly between the struts and decoratively nudge their way through. Trailing foliage, like a pretty variegated ivy, would also work well.

Garden bird feeder Every bird lover will adore a miniature woodland garden to hang from a bower or tree. When the flowers are over, they can be transplanted in the garden for next year, and the feeder can be filled with food for the birds to enjoy. Shallow-plant diminutive woodland bulbs, like snowdrops and crocuses (as shown), alongside flowering primroses. Cover the bulbs with wood bark and hang outdoors close to a window.

child of nature

Country-garden flowers make deliciously informal, pretty summer bouquets that will delight any child.

Butterfly net garden This tangle of flowers, spilling from a long-handled butterfly net, includes *Verbena bonariensis*, veronica and yarrow – all firm favourites with winged beauties. Buy a butterfly net and find a plastic container that fits snugly into the rim. Push a dome of chicken wire into the container, half-fill with water and arrange the flowers. Push the container tightly into the rim of the butterfly net just before presenting the gift.

Meadow mix A bucketful of meadow flowers and packets of seeds are ideal for a budding gardener. When planted, the seeds will bloom in a matter of weeks. Cornflowers, yarrow and camomile seeds are all good for a meadow mix.

clever cooks

For someone who loves to cook, there's an array of delicious and decorative herbs, fruits and flowers to choose from, as well as many gorgeous food-related containers.

Let them eat cake Fluted cake tins filled with edible flowers are an imaginative gift for a keen baker, inspiring them to create whimsical cakes decorated with sugared flowers.

Line the tins before planting up a miniature garden of pansies, concealing the soil with moss. Alternatively, use a chicken-wire frame to hold a lush posy of pinks and rosebuds that have been dipped in egg white and caster sugar to create cake decorations. Nasturtiums can dress up salads, a sprinkling of lavender flowers will make shortbread magical, and scented leaf geraniums will add flavour to jellies, drinks and biscuits. Interesting jelly moulds or mixing bowls are good alternative containers.

Buonissimo! Glossy red tomatoes, with their peppery scent, along with deliciously aromatic basil, are the essential ingredients for summery Italian-style pasta dishes. Here, they are presented in a colourful vintage tomato crate – a lucky junk-shop find. A supermarket pot of basil has been popped into a chunky ceramic mug, all ready to hold homemade tomato soup. The tomato plants are in individual pots that can be removed from the crate and left to ripen on a warm, sunny kitchen windowsill.

plant up the pestle and mortar with a fragrant
herb, such as basil, mint, rosemary or thyme

Herbs to go A smooth porcelain mortar planted up with a fragrant herb, such as basil, mint, rosemary or thyme, will be a welcome gift for any enthusiastic cook. Simply line the mortar with a piece of plastic liner or clingfilm, and pop in a pot of supermarket herbs. The herbs can be instantly snipped for cooking or garnishing, leaving the recipient with a beautiful and practical gift once the last leaf has been devoured.

Lemon tea Vintage caddies are unusual holders for flowers or plants, and can be put to good use afterwards as plant pots or storage jars. Fill a stoneware flour caddy with fresh flowers or, as shown above, an old tea caddy with a potted lemon tree (line the caddy before inserting the plant). Use the fruit in tea or (even better) an early-evening gin and tonic! Keep in a warm, sunny spot, and enjoy the glossy leaves and ripening fruits.

great gardeners

Don't be afraid to buy plants for garden lovers, but do be imaginative – it'll make all the difference.

Pretty maids all in a row A willow tool caddy is a pretty gift that can be dressed up decoratively to create a portable 'instant' garden. Line the inside of the basket with plastic liner or clingfilm, fill with bulb fibre, and plant up with a row of spring bulbs, like these cheerful, sunny *Narcissus* 'Tête-à-Tête' (alternatively, leave the bulbs in their pots and conceal the tops with moss). In summer, opt for a selection of pretty but diminutive cottage-garden plants – roses, lavender and columbines.

Beautifully practical Trugs and pots are invaluable in the garden – you can never have too many of them. Combine the two for a beautiful and useful gift. Plant up an assortment of terracotta pots with fragrant hyacinths, and embed them in a cushion of moss in the trug. The trug can be displayed as a single showpiece, or the pots can be removed and arranged individually.

perfectly potted

Watering can Using a can to water the garden is environmentally friendly as well as enjoyably therapeutic. Treat a green-fingered friend to a traditional-style enamelled-metal watering can, and decorate it with flowers. Choose blooms with large heads, like these lilac-tinged agapanthus, which burst forth from the neck of the can. Arrange them in a chicken-wire mesh, filling any gaps with frothy gypsophila. Don't forget to add water!

Hooked on classics A classically elegant urn, planted with topiary or a standard shrub like this beautiful azalea, adds style to any garden. The urn will weather beautifully, developing a fine antique patina. Plant it up with a piece of architectural topiary or a pretty shrub. Evergreens like this azalea, or box or yew, will give year-round enjoyment, but if you give a seasonal plant the urn can be replanted at regular intervals.

bookworms

A good read If you're a member of a book club, this would be the perfect present for anyone hosting a club meeting. The beautiful old books, with their gentle sepia tones, were found on a market stall. They have been tied in place around the four sides of a glass cube vase holding a bunch of strongly perfumed *Narcissus tazetta papyraceous*, or paperwhites. The papery sheaths of the narcissi are reminiscent of the faded pages of the books. The idea can also be adapted for music lovers, although you may need a larger vase and a concert-sized bouquet!

Bulbous bookends Two pretty, bulb-filled wicker baskets make a perfect pair of bookends. Fill a pair of long, low vases or little terracotta troughs – anything, really, which has a hole in it – with pretty bulbs, such as these double *Narcissus tazetta*. Glossy ceramics would work well for brightly coloured paperbacks, while ancient tomes like these are better suited to the tactile quality of wicker. Weigh down lightweight containers with stones before planting bulbs; otherwise they'll be top-heavy. And line your containers, or you'll ruin your library when watering!

sources

CREATIVE CONTAINERS

Remember that anything with a hole in it has the potential to be transformed into a container for a fantastic floral gift. Scour car-boot sales and antiques markets at home and abroad, and gather treasures to store away for fabulous future gifts. Some of my favourite sources for creative containers are as follows:

R.K. Alliston
173 New King's Road
London SW6 4SW
and at:
6 Quiet Street
Bath BA1 2JS
Mail order: 0845 130 5577
www.rkalliston.com
A wide and ever-changing selection of gardening goodies – trugs, log baskets, tool caddies, bird tables, lanterns, candles, enamelware and much more. Also a small selection of seasonal plants.

Atelier
26–28 Webb's Road
London SW11 6SF
020 7978 7733
Fabulous and sophisticated accessories for the home: felted bags, giant hurricane lanterns, delightful bowls and much more.

Braemar Antiques
113 Northcote Road
London SW11 6PW
020 7924 5628
From christening gowns and gifts to Victorian metal hatboxes, perfume bottles and vintage china. A real treasure trove.

The Dining Room Shop
62–64 White Hart Lane
London SW13 0PZ
020 8878 1020
www.thediningroomshop.co.uk
Perfect for vintage china, teapots, cups and saucers, jugs and other glass and ceramic vessels.

Green and Stone
259 King's Road
London SW3 5EL
020 7352 0837
www.greenandstone.com
Suppliers of artists' materials, as well as great desk accessories both old and new: inkwells, letter racks, pen holders, books, pens and more.

Living Vintage
113d Northcote Road
London SW11 6PW
020 7223 4440
Lovely items in vintage fabrics – knitted bootees, stockings and hats.

Marston and Langinger
192 Ebury Street
London SW1W 8UP
020 7881 5700
www.marston-and-langinger.com
Sophisticated glassware, lanterns and bowls, as well as a great selection of ceramic and metal pots.

Rosehip
226 Munster Road
London SW6 6AZ
020 7385 9638
www.rosehip.co.uk
Fabulous one-off vintage containers,
jugs, and mismatching cups and
saucers, as well as garden tables and
chairs, trugs, baskets and pots.

Talbot Walk Antiques Centre
The High Street
Ripley
Woking
Surrey GU23 6BB
01483 224884
www.talbotwalkantiques.com
Silverware, kitchenalia and garden
pots, cans and urns.

Tobias and The Angel
68 White Hart Lane
London SW13 OPZ
020 8296 0058
www.tobiasandtheangel.com
Inspirational finds for the home and
garden from times gone by.

ONE-STOP SHOPS

You can find flowers, plants and
imaginative containers at the
following stockists:

Appley Hoare Antiques and Interiors
30a Pimlico Road
London SW1 8LJ
020 7730 7317
www.appleyhoare.com
Inspirational antiques, with fabulous
vintage finds for home and garden –
cheese bells, dinner sets, vintage
seed tins, French fruit panniers and
stacks of old books, as well as flowers
and small plants.

The Chelsea Gardener
125 Sydney Street
London SW3 6NR
020 7352 5656
www.chelseagardener.com
A wide range of traditional containers
in wicker, glass and terracotta, as well
as plants and flowers.

Kraut and Rose
197 New King's Road
London SW6 4SR
020 7731 5168
A little jewel of a shop, with plants
flowers and accessories that are
perfect for creating floral gifts.

Petersham Nurseries
Off Petersham Road
Richmond
Surrey TW10 7AG
020 8940 5230
www.petershamnurseries.com
Accessories for the home and
garden, with many different inspiring
containers: fruit crates, glass cloches,
tin buckets, metal urns and troughs.
Also bulbs, plants and shrubs.

FLOWER MARKETS

Columbia Road Flower Market
Columbia Road
London E2 7QB
Sundays 8am to 2pm
Weekly plant and flower market.

Covent Garden Market
Nine Elms
London SW8 5NX
www.cgma.gov.uk/flowers.htm
A wonderful selection of plants and cut flowers, as well as florists' accessories and containers.

Flower Market
Market Precinct
Pershore Street
Birmingham B5 6UN

Manchester Flower Market
Piccadilly Gardens
Manchester
Held between 10am and 6pm every Thursday, Friday and Saturday.

South Yorkshire Fresh Produce and Flower Centre
Parkway Drive,
Sheffield S9 4WN
Flowers and fresh produce sold six days a week, Monday to Saturday.

CUT FLOWERS

Crocus
www.crocus.co.uk
Cut flowers and a selection of more unusual potted plants, including bougainvillea and lemon trees.

David Austin English Roses
01902 376301
www.davidaustinroses.com
Exquisite, fragrant English roses in delicious colours. Easy to arrange alone or with other flowers.

Sunflowers Direct
www.sunflowersdirect.co.uk
Fresh-cut flowers delivered boxed, with long stems ready to be cut down and arranged.

Tresco Flowers by Post
01720 422849
www.tresco.co.uk/tresco_flowers
Fabulous fragrant narcissi direct from the growers in the Scilly Isles, available from October to March.

BULBS

Broadleigh Bulbs
www.broadleighbulbs.co.uk
Great selection of seasonal bulbs.

Jacques Amand
www.jacquesamand.co.uk
Extensive selection of bulbs.

Miniature Bulbs UK
www.miniaturebulbs.co.uk
Fabulous, eye-catching miniature bulbs (great for little containers).

SEEDS

John Chambers
01933 652562
Wildflower seeds.

National Wildflower Centre
0151 738 1913
www.nwc.org.uk
Buy seeds online.

acknowledgments

Special thanks to Michelle for, as ever, working her magic with the camera; Lisa, her assistant; and everyone at Ryland Peters & Small who helped make *Floral Gifts* happen.

Thank you Tina, for being a wonderful friend and letting us ambush your home and garden; to Simon, who tirelessly stopped the car every time we passed an 'interesting' prop or garden shop; and to Teresa, who knows where to find even the most elusive of items.

Huge hugs to Lauren and Siena, my fabulous twin daughters, for squeezing into prop- and plant-filled cars on the school run, doing homework in a jungle, emptying toy boxes so floral gifts could be safely transported to locations, and to Lauren for modelling, while off school sick... Your turn next, Siena.

Most of all, thank you to all my friends and family, especially my dad, for giving me the desire and inspiration to create special gifts for people who are very special to me.